THE New Billable Hour

Advance Praise

In a profession where so many of us struggle with billing more hours AND trying to have work-life balance, *The New Billable Hour* approach is refreshing and practical. Ritu offers an ingenious, clear and easy-to-follow approach that even the busiest, most stressed-out lawyer can implement...and get results.

Beverly R. Davidek, Esq.,
best-selling author of *Happy Lawyer:*
The Art of Having It All Without Losing Your Mind

The New Billable Hour is making the most of an hour that will last you a lifetime. Well done, well written, and wonderful guidance for our fast paced world.

Dr. Ron Stotts, author of
Overscheduled by Success: A guide for Transformational
Leaders Too Busy to Create Their Next Dream

Working with lawyers on work/life balance issues for nearly decade (and being married to a workaholic attorney for 25 years, now) I can say Ritu Goswamy's fresh perspective is much-needed and beautifully delivered. She proves you can have legal career success and inner peace. I love how she used her own life experiences to craft an innovative way to thrive as an attorney. It should be required reading for lawyers.

Jill Farmer, author of *There's Not Enough Time... and Other Lies We Tell Ourselves*

When I first joined a law firm as a new attorney, I was discouraged at how little it seemed like we were actually able to use law to help people. I was okay working long hours and giving up my morning walk at first because I wanted to prove my capabilities, but I quickly grew dissatisfied with this arrangement—neither I, nor my clients, were benefiting. After arduous research and failed attempts to better serve my clients, I realized that if I was unhealthy, I was not able to bring my best work to my cases. If only Ritu Goswamy and *The New Billable Hour* had been available to me then it would have saved me so much research and agony! Every lawyer, especially those who feel like there is not enough time in the day to fulfill everyone's expectations, can benefit from Ritu's program. This book will not waste your time—it will save it. Take the time to check it out.

Meredith Holley, Esq., author of *Career Defense 101: Is your Career Safe from Sexism?*

The New Billable Hour, by Ritu Goswamy, shares a brilliant, simple, easy to implement system for transforming our relationship to the practice of law. As lawyers, we are encouraged to "just accept" an immense level of stress, denial of our own needs and all the mental and physical ailments which are eventually inevitable from such a work-life imbalance. When we are young, we think we are invincible and the stress may even feel "good", exciting, invigorating. But as a lawyer and judge for over 30 years, I am here to tell you that the effects *are* inevitable, and they sneak up on you. By the time you start to feel them, you feel too fundamentally exhausted to implement a self-care plan. Ritu's gift to the lawyering world is a system that even someone who has gone "too far" can implement with staggeringly beneficial results. I, for one, am so grateful for this gift!

Carol King, Esq., Attorney Consultant, Immigration Judge (ret.)

After 21 years of practicing law, every word in this book feels like a breath of fresh air. Thank you for writing this book, it's helping me to become a happier and a better attorney.

Ally Bolour, Esq.

Lawyers often find themselves in the predicament of losing time for themselves, in making time for others. Adding to that struggle is trying to re-establish that time in a meaningful way, if even for only a few minutes a day. Ms. Goswamy's book, *The New Billable Hour*, offers a straightforward, practical approach for attorneys to not only stake out a block of time every day to achieve greater balance and self-care, but also in a meaningful, readily-achievable way. Ms. Goswamy's approach is based on her own experience in the legal profession, as well as other long time practitioners, whose own experiences should tickle a twinge of familiarity in most attorney-readers. The commonality of experience helps create a firm foundation for Ms. Goswamy's practical, real-world advice in encouraging attorneys to engage in simple activities throughout their day-to-day to alleviate the frenetic self-sacrifice of the law. Ms. Goswamy's readily accessible approach, coupled with her well-written point-by-point explanation of her proposed "new billable hour," makes this a must-read for attorneys looking to achieve a greater work-life balance, if even only in a few minutes a day. All attorneys would benefit from a read of this book, and trying out Ms. Goswamy's "new billable hour."

Bryan A. Nickels, Esq.

The New Billable Hour by Ritu Goswamy is a fantastic short read for any lawyer who is searching for the tools to create more work life balance. I was immediately hooked by Ms. Goswamy's introduction-written so genuinely, I felt she was speaking directly to me. If Ms. Goswamy could so articulately describe the difficulties I face every day as a lawyer, I thought she surely must have the right guidance and she did. Thank you, Ms. Goswamy, for empowering lawyers with a concrete system of daily routines to keep their edge while finding balance in this busy world.

Dina Sokhn, Esq.

I love the practical examples of how I can build the new billable hour into my daily life. As a solo practitioner with small children, there never seems to be enough time to do everything, especially self-care. This book gives great suggestions for ways that I can set aside time to take care of myself and thus, become more productive. It is a quick, easy read and is written in a way that is conversational.

Kristin Boscia, Esq.

THE
New
Billable
Hour

Bill More Hours, Be More Productive
and Still Have Work-Life Balance

Ritu Goswamy, Esq.

NEW YORK

LONDON • NASHVILLE • MELBOURNE • VANCOUVER

THE New Billable Hour
Bill More Hours, Be More Productive and Still Have Work-Life Balance

Published in New York, New York, by Morgan James Publishing in partnership with Difference Press. Morgan James is a trademark of Morgan James, LLC. www.MorganJamesPublishing.com

The Morgan James Speakers Group can bring authors to your live event. For more information or to book an event visit The Morgan James Speakers Group at www.TheMorganJamesSpeakersGroup.com.

ISBN 978-1-64279-127-3 paperback
ISBN 978-1-64279-128-0 eBook
Library of Congress Control Number: 2018906776

Cover Design by:
Rachel Lopez
www.r2cdesign.com

Interior Design by:
Bonnie Bushman
The Whole Caboodle Graphic Design

In an effort to support local communities, raise awareness and funds, Morgan James Publishing donates a percentage of all book sales for the life of each book to Habitat for Humanity Peninsula and Greater Williamsburg.

Get involved today! Visit
www.MorganJamesBuilds.com

To my devoted parents, my very first teachers, who always supported me in all of my unconventional choices.

In memory of Ted Sapeta, my high school business teacher and mentor, who always believed in me and my potential.

Table of Contents

	Introduction: My Story	*xiii*
Chapter 1	Being a Lawyer	1
Chapter 2	The Old Billable Hour	15
Chapter 3	The New Billable Hour	21
Chapter 4	Lesson One: Meditation, .1 Hours	29
Chapter 5	Lesson Two: Lunch Break, .2 Hours	37
Chapter 6	Lesson Three: Morning Routine, .2 Hours	49
Chapter 7	Lesson Four: Night Routine, .2 Hours	57
Chapter 8	Lesson Five: Movement (with Breath), .2 hours	65
Chapter 9	Lesson Six: Connecting with Nature, .1 Hours	71
Chapter 10	Competence and Diligence	77
	Conclusion	81
	Acknowledgments	*85*
	About the Author	*89*
	Thank You	*91*

Introduction
My Story

Like you, I went to law school wanting to make a difference and to change the world. I wanted to use my privilege to be able to give back in some way and have a challenging and rewarding career that would sustain me. I wanted a career in which I could share my gifts with the world. I knew I was smart enough, and a career in the law fascinated me. I saw a lawyer as someone who helped people through their problems. I saw lawyers as advocates, people who gave a voice to those who did not have one. I saw lawyers as professionals who helped people who were in some kind of conflict navigate the systems available to them to get some kind of resolution.

And then my recent college graduate self went to law school and had a rude awakening. Somehow those hopes and dreams were not readily apparent in our studies of case law and statutes. And the style of teaching, as well as the environment designed to foster competition, didn't help. Even though the process was tough, and I saw classmates drop out, I stayed the course, graduated, and passed the bar. I had a career as a public interest lawyer in the nonprofit sector and then started my own law practice. My career as a lawyer has been fulfilling and meaningful.

But I still did not understand how the profession could be so callous and harsh. I found myself being ashamed of being a lawyer, of not wanting to say what I did for a living because of what people would think. I noticed that when I said I was a lawyer, people would involuntarily jump back, widen their eyes, and decide certain things about me. They would say things like, "Oh, you are a lawyer—I understand now."

The education of lawyers and the professional lifestyle is obviously stressful and unforgiving. The pressures and demands of practicing law are unique: You take on your clients' problems in addition to your own. I know that you know what I am talking about. The clients hire you to solve their problems, and helping another person means all that goes with that. You take those problems with you wherever you go. You think about those problems night and day.

Anyone hiring you is going through some conflict or transition. That person is seeking a professional to help him through a process he doesn't understand. He is giving up some control to allow you, the expert and professional, to guide him and help him get to the other side. When people are wronged, they will go into survival mode and seek to right the situation in some way. So then, on top of helping someone with his problem or transition, you are charged with the role of getting him the vindication his emotions require at the time. Now you are fighting for your client to be right in what is likely a complicated and messy situation, when you might not even agree.

Ethics, anyone? To review, you are taking on other people's problems and emotions and innate need to be right and "win"—when you yourself might not even feel aligned with what you are doing. To cope, often you separate yourself from the work and use

Through my yoga studies, I became aware of its sister science, Ayurveda. According to Ayurveda, we are urged to proactively maintain our health instead of reacting to illness. It teaches that, in order to be our best selves, we need to care for ourselves and stay in balance.

When I talk with other lawyers, their concern about engaging in self-care is that they will lose their edge as lawyers. We lawyers love our edge, don't we? I could not find any guidance about how to practice self-care according to this ancient wisdom in modern times.

I was drawn to learn next about lifestyle design. I figured I would learn how to work in fewer hours so that I had more time for self-care, so I sought out resources for being more productive and efficient. I picked up Tim Ferriss's *The 4-Hour Workweek*, and his energy fueled my tweaking my work hours so that I could have more time for self-care and a personal life!

And of course, working fewer hours does allow for more self-care time. And working fewer hours does allow for more time for a personal life, whatever that is for you. Great, I thought. Now I can help others do this. But lawyers don't necessarily want to work fewer hours.

Lawyers have billable-hour requirements. Lawyers have loans and bills to pay and perhaps families to provide for. Lawyers need to bill *more* hours. I get it.

You want a life, but *billing* more hours is your priority. You are interested in taking care of yourself. You know that, as you age, practicing law is taking a toll on your health. You know that if you don't make some changes, your ability to practice law may be in jeopardy. And, even though you are highly intelligent and capable, you can't figure out why self-care is so difficult.

Well, in the last couple of years of devoting myself to an Ayurvedic lifestyle while still practicing law, I have learned a few things. I have learned how to Ayurveda-hack my life to get the nuggets I need to stay aligned and balanced. And I have learned that, in order to be the sharp, edgy lawyer I want to be, I have to allow myself to get imbalanced! Yes, to do the job we do, we need to go deep into action mode.

The hacks are to know how to get back into balance when we purposefully get imbalanced—and spend fewer hours doing it so that we can *bill more* hours. Using everything I have learned from yoga, Ayurveda, business books, and actually following these practices, I have created a system for your self-care that takes only *one billable hour* per day. This is the New Billable Hour™.

Chapter 1
Being a Lawyer

If there were no bad people,
there would be no good lawyers.
–Charles Dickens

I was in immigration court waiting my turn and observing another hearing. The attorney did not bring her clients, who were children attending school at the time. The judge was furious and screaming at the attorney. She said it was the lawyer's job to bring her clients and it was required they be there. The lawyer said she had hoped their presence could be waived because they were children and in school. The judge responded: "Your clients pay you to be paranoid."

Recently, I have been hearing many lawyers lament that we must take on our clients' problems. In a recent group consulting program for lawyers I facilitated, the participants all said they wanted to feel less responsible for their clients' problems. Lawyers also tell me that they are worried about getting in trouble with their state licensing organizations for not being competent lawyers if they are not completely consumed by their cases. You don't want to mess up your cases. You don't want to take too long or miss deadlines. And this leads to feeling guilty.

You know that your clients are taking over your time to your detriment. You know that you are a different person now than you were before law school. Remember when you actually thought of yourself as your own person, before you took on clients? I work for myself now, and yes, think about my clients often and make sure they are looked after. But I remember when I had jobs and worked for someone else. When I would leave a job, I *still* felt guilty for leaving my clients behind. Even though they would get a new lawyer, I felt like I was abandoning them. What is this about?

The legal profession requires that we zealously and competently advocate for our clients. Somewhere along the way in law school and our careers, we are made to feel that we are not good enough and not spending enough time working. This feeling is universal. Seems like no one told us you would feel like this, and so you feel alone here. But you are not alone, and it is completely normal.

Here you are: a smart, highly educated professional who has been trained to worry about other people's lives when you cannot possibly control what will happen. And if you don't believe in your clients or yourself, you suffer more. You suffer from guilt—how interesting is that?

You, as a lawyer, who advocates for your clients to be presumed innocent, automatically decide you are *guilty*. And the punishment is to work more, worry more, and beat yourself up if circumstances don't go the way you (and your clients) would like. You know that the client chose his destiny and possibly made mistakes. You know the system is riddled with its own problems and the innocent do get caught up in it.

So how did *you* take on the guilt for a broken system, and clients who make mistakes? Deep down, you believe there is justice in this chaotic world. You have to, right? If you didn't believe in these systems, your role would be irrelevant. I know that, even after so many years of being shown the ugly truths of the legal and political systems, I still believe in justice. I still believe in laws, structure, and rules. I believe that these systems are here to help us, keep us functioning together, and resolve conflict. I also believe that lawyers are necessary for the whole thing to work. Lawyers make laws and enforce and interpret them. Lawyers also fight against the systems when the laws are not working anymore or are unjust, discriminatory, and harmful.

I know you also believe in the law; that is why you chose this profession. You want to have a meaningful career in this profession. You know deep down that this work is something you are good at and enjoy. You like the status of being a professional and ability to be an expert for people who need it. You are satisfied with the fees and income you command because of your worth.

Then why do you feel so *guilty*? What have you done? You are not corrupt and stealing from your clients and not providing the work. You are not trying to cut corners and then bill for more than the work required. But you still feel guilty for not working enough. For me, outside comparisons influence my feelings of guilt. I must be doing something wrong if I am not doing the same as my colleague, for example.

You probably come from a hardworking family like I do. My parents immigrated to the United States for the "American dream" of working hard for what you earn. They wanted their children to be successful. Well, that is a source of guilt too! Who knows what came first—were we prone to feeling guilty and so we chose to be lawyers, or did becoming lawyers make us feel guilty? It doesn't matter, because here we are.

We are in this together, and to make any changes in the legal profession we must help each other. Let's not get competitive about who works more or who feels guiltier. If you can understand that we are all feeling this unnecessary guilt as lawyers, you can take steps to alleviate that suffering. You can see more clearly that you need to do this important healing work and have more sustainability in the profession.

You already know about the health crisis in the legal profession, that the incidence of anxiety, depression, substance abuse, and myriad lifestyle-related diseases is rapidly increasing. In the extreme cases, the media reports suicides and drug overdoses among lawyers. I read about a local lawyer found after a lethal drug overdose next to his lawyer notes. So he was lawyering literally until the end.

The 2017 report "The Path to Lawyer Well-Being: Practical Recommendations For Positive Change" by the National Task Force on Lawyer Well-Being summarized the results of a study done by the American Bar Association:

> It found that between 21 and 36 percent [of lawyers in the study] qualify as problem drinkers, and that approximately 28 percent, 19 percent, and 23 percent are struggling with some level of depression, anxiety, and stress, respectively. The

parade of difficulties also includes suicide, social alienation, work addiction, sleep deprivation, job dissatisfaction, a "diversity crisis," complaints of work-life conflict, incivility, a narrowing of values so that profit predominates, and negative public perception…. The budding impairment of many of the future generation of lawyers should be alarming to everyone. Too many face *less productive* [emphasis added], less satisfying, and more troubled career paths.

So what do we do? William Shakespeare's *Henry VI* includes the famous line, "The first thing we do, let's kill all the lawyers." But that would not be practical. As long as we have laws and conflict (necessary for any society, I think), we need lawyers to help. And if you run yourself into the ground and put your clients' and employers' needs above your own, you will be no good to anyone.

I know you already know this. And I know that this problem is bigger than you can handle. In fact, you don't have much control over the current state of the profession. Actually, you are just trying to get through the day. You are just trying to get your billable hours completed and to do the best job you can.

But there is a voice whispering to you that something is not right. Perhaps your physical health is declining, especially as you age. Maybe the voice telling you to slow down is getting louder. Could it be that you are looking for another way to balance yourself so that you can keep practicing law? You want to be a good lawyer *and* have a satisfying personal life. Further, you want to contribute to your community and be there for your family.

You desire these things, but the drive to work more is just so strong. *You don't even have enough hours in the day* to meet your billable requirement. You are struggling with what you have to do and just cannot take on any more. You are intrigued by the idea of having more work-life balance but overwhelmed by the thought of doing more in an already full life.

You are an ambitious, strong-willed person. You are successful in your career and want to continue to excel. You hear about self-care but you just don't have enough time. You would feel guilty for doing it anyway. That said, you don't feel great in your body, your mind is not as sharp as it used to be, and there is that whisper that something is imbalanced deep within you.

You are not alone; let me tell you about Jonathan:

Jonathan, 37, is married to Anna and they have 2 daughters, who are 5 and 2. They met in law school, but Anna stopped practicing law when their first daughter was born. Now she is a stay-at-home mom, and Jonathan supports the family by practicing at a small civil litigation firm in Boston, MA.

Jonathan loves the outdoors and majored in environmental studies in college. He was an avid biker, hiker, and rock climber, and loved to backpack and camp out. He and Anna had that in common when they met—their love of the great outdoors.

Jonathan went to law school right out of college because he loved the ads from the nonprofit organization Earth Justice, which said, "When the earth needs a good lawyer." He was motivated by social justice and truly wanted to make a difference to protect the planet. He was especially concerned about open spaces being destroyed by big business. Jonathan went to law school to save the world.

But when he got to law school, it was a different story. The competition was strange to him, but, being highly intelligent and organized, he was able to excel. After the first year of law school, he gradually stopped doing the outdoor activities he loved. He and Anna were so busy with law school responsibilities that they hardly spent time away from the library, much less on an outdoor adventure. They figured that, when they were done with school, they would pick up those activities again.

He took a class on environmental law and looked for internships in the field, but the pay was not what he needed to pay back his school loans. So, while in law school, he accepted a job at a prestigious law firm doing civil litigation in the areas of contracts, land use, and real estate.

In the 10 years since graduation, the work has been challenging and satisfying for Jonathan in many ways. But the lawyer lifestyle has taken a toll on him. Running has been Jonathan's mainstay for exercise and stress relief. He runs every morning before going to work. Anna knows that no one can get in the way of his morning ritual of running and drinking a green smoothie. At home, the family eats healthy organic meals because Anna can prepare them. They take vacations a couple of times of year and have family outings on Sunday afternoons.

But he never got back into his other outdoor activities. He works most days of the week; even though he is with his family for dinner and on the weekend, Jonathan does go into the office or works from home for a few hours on both Saturday and Sunday. And after he has dinner with his family and the kids are in bed, he usually works for a few more hours at night. His phone is on him at all times and is the last thing he looks to at night and first thing when he wakes up.

He and Anna do have date nights and spend time together when they can. But she understands the lawyer lifestyle and is grateful she was able to quit her job and get out of it. So she does not mind that Jonathan works so much, since that is what he needs to do to be a lawyer. He is a great father when he is with the girls and he makes sure everyone is cared for.

Jonathan is aware he works a lot, but he has become used to it by now. He wakes up early for his run and green smoothie, and then drinks Diet Cokes all day at the office. He buys them by the case. He rarely takes a lunch break, but when he does, he'll have something light like a salad. He enjoys peanut M&Ms and has them at his side to munch on at all times.

Litigation is stressful because of the deadlines and client demands. On top of that, the partners of the firm are always on him to bill more hours. So Jonathan is constantly in hyperalert mode. His brain is always going, trying to solve problems. He never turns this mode off, and doesn't even know how to relax. He has not slept well in years, has regular bouts of severe stomach pain, and his back and neck spasm to give him regular headaches. For his stomach pains, he has gone to the emergency room several times, and the doctors tell him it is due to stress.

To cope, Jonathan has found that having a drink, or two or three, when he gets home from work helps him relax and numb the pain. Drinking helps him unwind and fall asleep. Or sometimes he takes sleeping pills. But, inevitably, around 3 a.m., he will wake up suddenly with his mind going again. He can eventually fall back asleep, but he is not rested in the morning. And then he starts his day all over again.

Jonathan thinks about getting older as he approaches 40, and is worried his health is just going to get worse. He worries about being able to financially provide for his family. But mostly he is worried about his use of alcohol. Alcoholism is so common among his peers, he would not dare talk to anyone about it. And Anna picked up the habit of drinking in law school, so she will usually at least have a glass of wine with him.

Jonathan feels like he is on a hamster wheel of constantly being "on" and in "work mode." Even though he knows he should take more time off, he is addicted to working since that is what he knows.

Of course, this "billable hour" is not an hour as you know it in the rest of your life. It is only the actual time spent doing lawyer work on your client's case. As my law school classmate explained to me when he had a summer job at a prestigious law firm, there is so much you have to do that is not billable, like billing your time! I found that amusing. However, it is true that you have to do so much as a lawyer that is not billable, including client development and continuing education. If you work for someone else, you may have paralegal help and not have to worry about bringing in clients, but if you have your own firm, you know that the business development work often eclipses the billable lawyer work.

Okay, so if you have a law firm job with an average billable-hour requirement, let's take a look at that. Lawyers have billable hour requirements from 1,500 to 2,500 or more. So let's use 2,000. This lawyer—maybe it's you—has to bill 2,000 hours per year to earn his salary. So that is 40 hours per week. Well, that's not so bad.

Wait a minute! That's 40 billable hours *every* week, for the *whole* year. If you take 2 weeks' vacation (I hope you do at least that!), then there are only 50 working weeks in the year.

And I think I am not exaggerating when I say that sometimes it takes double the number of hours in the office to earn your billable time. One lawyer told me that he would find himself in the office for 12 hours, only to bill 6. And then there is the ugly truth no one wants to talk about: adjusting the hours afterward. By adjusting, I mean decreasing your hours because you are embarrassed about how much time you spent on a case. This "underbilling" is a pervasive problem among lawyers.

Furthermore, I recently had a conversation with a partner at a law firm, and he casually told me that the industry collection rate for billable hours is about 75%! Wait, so the hours you bill are not all collected? For the bottom line of a business, this collection rate has to be accounted for in the hourly rate for each attorney and in the billable-hour requirement. A 2017 legal trends report by the Clio legal practice management company found that, in an 8-hour day, the average lawyer only collects 1.6 hours of billable time. The report goes on to ask, "What happens to the 6 missing hours?"

The solo self-employed or small-firm lawyer is doing his best to bill his time. But again, this lawyer is also not collecting everything he bills. And of course, what we collect is used to pay expenses (which are many for the lawyer), and we are obviously taxed on our income. There is a growing trend to charge a flat rate in several areas of law including criminal, estate planning, family, and immigration. This works better for collection, but we have to be careful about charging the right amount since events can happen in the case that will result in us working more hours than planned, and then we have the same problem, of not really earning the billable hours we put in.

In the immigration field, where I practice, some lawyers charge flat rates, some hourly, and some (like me) are doing a hybrid, with a flat rate and the ability to charge hourly for work that goes beyond the agreement. The bottom line is that you charge for your services by the hour, no matter how you slice it. This billable hour is broken down into .1-hour or 6-minute increments, and that influences how you see *all* hours. Everything seems like a non-billable distraction from the main event—the billable hour!

Here you are, a highly intelligent educated person, with the ability to analyze complex situations for your clients. But you cannot get past this billable-hour situation. You need to be working as much as you can for maximum productivity, right? And thank goodness people (like you) who choose to be lawyers are type-A overachievers who love to work. Because working is what you do! You work so much that you have no life. Well, you have a life, but not that "work-life balance" you always hear about.

How can you take any time to relax when there is barely enough time to meet your billable-hours requirement and your other non-billable work requirements? And you have to keep up with your personal responsibilities, right? This billable-hour system sets you up to fail. You cannot see time in the same way. Your time is not yours and it is not really even time. It is this idea that your worth is measured in time, but as we know, it is not a direct relationship.

No wonder you don't have time for things you did before law school. No wonder you are always at the office and bringing work home. No wonder you are very judicious with the "free" time you have. *You are in this constant state of feeling you don't have enough time.* And in many ways, with this billable-hour system, you don't. *You are wishing that you had more hours in the day to bill clients.* So it is understandable that you don't get to the gym as often as you would like. How time-consuming! And who has time to eat lunch? That is a pesky waste of time in the middle of the day. I get it. There just isn't enough time in the day do everything you need to do.

If you're dreaming of a better way where there *is* enough time, I'm here to tell you there is! Keep reading to learn about how the New Billable Hour can work for you.

Chapter 3
The New Billable Hour

Finish each day and be done with it. You have done what you could. Some blunders and absurdities no doubt crept in; forget them as soon as you can. Tomorrow is a new day. You shall begin it serenely and with too high a spirit to be encumbered with your old nonsense.

–Ralph Waldo Emerson

Y ou are in the right place. In this book, I explain a system that turns the old billable hour requirement on its head. I propose billing just one hour per day, every day, to your lawyer self before you bill your precious time to clients. In essence, you become your own client.

This revolutionary act forces you to shift what you thought was possible in your relationship to time. Your schedule is full and you can't take anything away from your billable hours. In fact, you want to bill *more* hours. In order to increase your time and energy for your other clients, you will add time serving yourself as your own client.

As a lawyer, you have been trained to flow against nature. As a result, your life is out of balance. If you can gradually get back into flow, you will understand that time is not what you think it is. Time is expansive, and there is enough of it. Further, your role in influencing the lives of your clients is infinite, irrespective of the "billable hours" or worry you put into a case.

By putting your attention on yourself first, you will free up the attention and time you desperately need to help your clients. This means more focused time, i.e., "billable hours" for your clients, which leads to happy clients, happy boss, happy lawyer! Remember the ABA Wellness Study that projected that the legal profession in its current state would lead to less productive lawyers?

You will be a leader in creating a new *more productive* approach to lawyering.

When I teach this system to lawyers, they also do not have time to add anything more to their busy schedules. They feel guilty about not working on their clients' cases. They do not prioritize their own well-being above their clients' needs. But these lawyers also know that they are out of balance. They know they need to feel better about themselves and their work. They try to do "self-care" but get frustrated since they cannot implement lifestyle changes on their own. They just want concrete steps to help them feel better and gain control of their time.

First, this system is not about "self-care" in the way you think. Activities such as shopping, eating unhealthy foods, and consuming alcohol are indulgences that merely distract you from the real issue of imbalance. No matter how much you distract yourself, nothing is going to change that you work more than you should, only to feel guilty for not working enough. In fact, in excess, the distractions and indulgences will lead to addiction and other physical or mental health problems.

So where does that leave you? With this system, you will develop the simple, time-honored practice of daily routines that will address all the issues you have with imbalance. In other words, by putting yourself first, as your own main client who requires just one billable hour per day, you shift your attention away from guilt and onto being your best self. Because the time is billable, you must be efficient. Because it is for yourself by yourself, you cannot blame anyone or feel guilty. It is not possible.

Here is the 6-step system of the New Billable Hour:

Step 1: Meditate (.1 hours)
Step 2: Take a real lunch break (.2 hours)
Step 3: Engage with an energizing morning routine (.2 hours)
Step 4: Relax with a grounding night routine (.2 hours)
Step 5: Incorporate movement with breath (.2 hours)
Step 6: Connect with nature (.1 hours)

For the next six weeks, you will incorporate one step into your life until you have learned all of them. So in week one, you only bill .1 hours per day for meditation. Then week two, you will start also billing for the lunch break, for a total of .3 hours per day. In week three, you begin billing for the morning routine, which makes .5 hours. In week four, you will add the night routine, for a daily total of .7 hours. Then, in week five, you'll be billing for movement, for a total of .9 hours. In week six, you will also bill for connecting with nature and bill one complete hour, the New Billable Hour, to yourself before you bill clients.

You will bill the New Billable Hour to yourself every day, 7 days a week. You will bill it to yourself on a regular workday, but also when you are traveling, at home, when you are working long hours, and when you are in crisis. When you are in crisis, it is *more* important to bill this hour. It may be the only hour you bill that day, and it will save your life. There is a story about Mahatma Gandhi (he was a lawyer, by the way) that his followers were briefing him about his schedule, and he informed them that he needed one hour per day for meditation. When they said, "You are too busy to meditate an hour every day!" he responded that he then needed *two* hours of meditation every day.

When you are so busy and falling apart that you cannot function, that is when this system will pay off. Just when you are about to have a breakdown because you cannot concentrate on your cases, you will bill yourself the New Billable Hour, and things will become clear.

The New Billable Hour will balance and align you in this chaotic world. When the thoughts in your head and the tragedies around you seem too much to bear, you will retreat into the safety of this billable hour that you have created for yourself. This billable hour, once you take some time to learn it by asserting discipline over yourself, will become automatic. You won't even remember not having that new hour to bill. The routines and activities will be natural and comfortable.

That being said, change is difficult. I promise you will not like this change to the New Billable Hour. You will not want to do it, come up with reasons not to, and resist along the way. That's okay. Actually, it's perfect. Changing your habits should be met with resistance. That is what we do for safety. But you are a stronger opposing force, dear lawyer! You will win over the resistance if you want it enough. Do you want it enough?

In the chapters ahead, I will break down each step so you will understand better what you need to do. You get so much information thrown at you as it is, so I will teach only what is necessary to achieve your goal. You can definitely do it, just as other lawyers before you have done it.

In implementing the New Billable Hour in your life, please follow these rules:

Rule 1: Try your best to bill what you are supposed to bill. Set the intention and make the effort.

Rule 2: No double billing...yet. Initially, make sure you bill each separate activity for the time required. If you do them simultaneously, just add the required time. For example, if you meditate at the beach, you can bill for both meditation and connecting with nature. But for now, you must bill .1 hours for meditation and .1 hours for connecting with nature. So, .2 hours of meditating at the beach, get it?

Rule 3: Restart from the beginning every day. You will bill the New Billable Hour every day, but at the end of the day you are done—whether you were a superstar that day and billed your hour with ease, whether you struggled, or whether you even finished. At the end of the day, go to sleep knowing you tried your best. Then you restart the next day anew. You cannot make up missed hours or bill ahead. This is an exercise in real time, in being present, in trusting that you tried your best, and in believing that *you are good enough*. As long as you put your billable hour first and try your best, you get credit for the hour.

You now have the framework for how to use this book. With each lesson, remember the rules above and be gentle with yourself. Even though incorporating this New Billable Hour into your daily life will be hard at first, the payoff in time, productivity, money, happiness, health, and peace of mind will be well worth it.

Chapter 4
Lesson One:
Meditation, .1 Hours

In the beginner's mind there are many possibilities, but in the expert's there are few.
—Shunryu Suzuki

When I was a young lawyer in my 20s, I wanted to learn how to meditate. I was overwhelmed with my work and life and had heard that meditation would help me. So, naturally, I found a book to teach myself. The book that started this all was *Zen Mind, Beginner's Mind* by Shunryu Suzuki. I learned from this book that the point of meditation was to learn to approach everything with a beginner's mind, not knowing what would happen next.

I decided I was going to meditate for five minutes every day, and I learned to do it in the Zen tradition, which comes from Japan. I sat in silence on a cushion on the floor and faced a blank wall. I did it all by myself. Those five minutes when I started to meditate were terrible. I wanted to jump out of my skin, and I felt bad about myself. But I still did it every single day, since I have a lot of self-discipline. And then it got easier, and I increased the time. This practice has changed my life. I have learned how to calm down my mind, to reach different states of consciousness, and I have so much more clarity about my life purpose.

Your first lesson for the New Billable Hour is to meditate for six minutes a day. I prefer you sit quietly and do nothing, but you can use any tools that you need to start your own meditation practice. Meditation may be scary for you. You were born as a peaceful creature and then learned to worry as you grew up. Then in law school you learned to worry about things you hadn't even known you should be worrying about. On top of this, many lawyers already have the personality of someone who worries. So all that conditioning is there.

When you sit still quietly and don't do anything, alarms start going off. The human body and mind give you messages and reasons why you shouldn't meditate, and that feels terrible. You may even feel like you are going to die. If you do have something like a panic attack, please stop. But if you just feel uncomfortable, see how long you can literally sit with that feeling. With practice, your stamina will increase.

A big fear for me with meditation has always been that it will make me lose my edge as a lawyer. You think that what makes you a good lawyer is being on the edge of anxiety and stress, that they fuel your motivation to do your best work. You may have to step away from that edge. But there is a new and different edge on the horizon, which will bring increased productivity. It is going to be different for each person. There is going to be this new opening up of time and space for you.

I suggest you allow yourself to get soft and vulnerable. You already know how to do hard things. So gently set a timer and sit in silence, and you are done. But if you need some help, use a mobile app or recording for a guided meditation. And, while six minutes is an ideal time period for this exercise, you can meditate for 5 or 10 minutes if that works better for you. The exact amount of time is not the point. The point is to develop a practice or habit to meditate *daily*.

The best time to meditate is in the morning right before sunrise (or close to that time). I meditate first thing when I wake up, after my personal hygiene. The most spiritual time in the day is when night becomes day. You can also meditate before you fall asleep. Your quality of sleep will increase with this nightly practice. Of course, meditating in both the morning and night is beneficial, and you can do 3 minutes each session for your daily 6 minutes of meditation.

Also, it is helpful to meditate in the same place every day. Your anxiety will decrease because your body will learn the habit of sitting in that place at that time of day. That place can be your bed—if you sit up. I have, especially in hotels and new places, meditated in my bed. If you want to do this, sit up and set a timer for six minutes. Your meditation for the day will be finished before you leave the bed.

If you have other people in your life, like partners and children, you will have to negotiate agreements and support from them. One client told me that, if she got up just a little earlier and kept it short, she could have her spouse take care of the children so she could meditate. You can also meditate first thing when you get to your office, to set the tone for the day. This may not be realistic at first, though, since when you get to the office you are already in another mindset. I think you can more easily do this later, when you have mastered this skill away from the office.

A client explained to me that, while she loved doing self-care in the mornings, she felt guilty because she was not working. She felt that she should be at the office as early as possible. She explained what most of us are struggling with, that time devoted to herself was time away from something else (like work). She wanted the space for both. Let me reassure you that, by devoting time to both work and self-care, your productivity will increase exponentially.

One reason you resist taking time for self-care is that you compare yourself to other lawyers. "Well, since Joe is working 80 hours per week, he must be a better lawyer!" you think. "Surely Joe does not need to spend time doing self-care." But what if you agreed to take one hour per day to care for yourself and you helped other lawyers do this instead of getting competitive? If we all do this, we can change the profession. This will help our clients, help us, and help how people see us. It is all intertwined.

I have a client who I will call Bob. Bob is a well-known criminal defense attorney who often takes on murder trials. He works seven days a week, and he says it is relaxing going to the office on weekends. But Bob also likes to be stressed! He sought out my services because he heard about meditation's numerous benefits and wanted to learn how to do it. During our sessions, he would sit in my office and close his eyes while I led a guided meditation exercise, usually focusing on the breath. As a longtime yoga practitioner and instructor, I use the breath as a tool to settle both the body and the mind. Bob liked my meditations and would sometimes do them on his own.

Bob explained to me that, every night when he goes to bed, he spends about five minutes meditating before he falls asleep. He said, that when he does that, something happens. He feels a different level of consciousness that goes beyond thinking about cases or other things he needs to do. "I don't know how to describe it. I am concentrating on my breathing and thinking about nothing else." He said it is not like being quiet and reading or listening to music or watching television. It is different. He had only been doing this for one month to six weeks at the time, so this "place" was new. He felt like he was at the top of the hill waiting to come down. He could feel that there is something down there that other people talk about. He could imagine being in a place where he would feel more empathy, notice beautiful natural things, do six hours of work in four, be a kinder person, and be mindful (even though he says that he does not know what that means).

Bob reported that it was not hard to practice five minutes of meditation every night. He incorporated it into his life. And he realized, he told me, that, "being stressed has disadvantages too." He told me how, in the past, he would be working on a case and would remember that he had some piece of information somewhere that would help him. He could waste four hours looking for this information when it would take 30 minutes to recreate it. He asserted, "I am finding... *a greater belief in my ability to create rather than copy.*"

The benefits of meditation are well documented, and the studies continue to prove that meditation can improve many aspects of your life. Meditation reduces stress, improves concentration, encourages a healthy lifestyle, increases self-awareness and acceptance, slows aging, and induces relaxation that benefits cardiovascular and immune health. These benefits are achieved soon after you begin a regular, consistent meditation practice. So why wait any longer?

Chapter 5
Lesson Two:
Lunch Break, .2 Hours

First we eat, then we do everything else.
–M.F.K. Fisher

Currently, do you take a lunch break from your work? Do you even eat lunch at all? You may just "forget" to eat lunch. If you do eat lunch, you are probably working while you eat—reading email, making phone calls, or writing briefs.

I had a client, who we'll call Michelle, and she shared in our group program that she only ate lunch when she had plans with someone else. Otherwise she would not take a break and not eat. When I asked her why, she said she did not like to eat alone. She was born a twin, and she doesn't like to do anything alone. She was used to eating with her sister or her family. They always ate their meals together. It had been a problem her entire life that when she was alone, she did not eat. As a lawyer, she easily worked through lunchtime so she didn't have to worry about it.

To do this exercise, Michelle said she set a timer both on her phone and Fitbit to remind her it was time to eat. She ate lunch every day the week she started, and she has done it every day since. She said she looks forward to having 12 minutes each day just to eat. I tell you her story to illustrate that changing your lifestyle is very possible by working this program.

This week's exercise is a continuation of paying attention to yourself. People think that a lunch break has to be a full hour. No, it doesn't. If you don't always eat lunch, this lesson is to make sure you eat. If you can focus on just eating your food mindfully, it will take you about 10–15 minutes. I do this all the time now. Before, I would have my food with me but do other things rather than eat it. Then I would look at the time and a client would be coming in 15 minutes! So I learned to stop everything I am doing at that moment and eat for about 12 minutes. That's how I realized this was a good time hack.

Since we are talking about lunch, I would like to formally introduce you to the science of Ayurveda. This Sanskrit word translates to "science of life." The *Merriam-Webster Dictionary* defines Ayurveda as "a form of alternative medicine that is the traditional system of medicine of India and seeks to treat and integrate body, mind, and spirit using a comprehensive, holistic approach especially by emphasizing diet, herbal remedies, exercise, meditation, breathing, and physical therapy." In this book, I am drawing upon this alternative system of medicine to help you balance your life so that you can be a more productive lawyer.

In the Ayurvedic system, the main meal of the day is lunch. But you probably skip it because you don't have time for a *lunch hour*. This is why I created a 12-minute break for you to nourish yourself in the middle of the day. If you slow down in the middle of the day and eat a meal for about 10–15 minutes, you will reap the benefits of a balanced lifestyle.

For this exercise, do not be too concerned about what you eat. It is a good idea to eat nutritious food, and snacking on candy or a soda does not count, but at this stage, there is no need to get caught up in what you are eating. But it is very important to eat a meal at lunchtime.

The middle of the day is when your digestive fire is at its strongest. When you don't pay attention to that fire, your health will suffer the consequences, which can show up as ulcers, acid reflux, and other inflammatory illnesses. All of that can happen because you are not feeding yourself at the right time. Therefore, this week's lesson is to eat nutritious food, in the middle of the day, every day. It may take a while to get used to, but you will develop that habit.

If your barrier is that you don't have food with you when you go to work, you can figure out a time hack to that. Obviously, the 12 minutes is the billable time, and buying and preparing your food is not billable. So keep all of that as simple as you can while you develop this habit of eating every day. One option is that you can make extra dinner and put it aside for your lunch (not leftovers, but intentionally put some away for the next day before you serve your meal). Or you can outsource that task and buy a prepared lunch.

If you want to take a full hour-long lunch break, that's awesome. And if you want to go to a restaurant, of course do that! But that is above and beyond what is required for this exercise. You are allowed to do that; you don't have to eat lunch in 12 minutes. This is just the minimum. But I am going to make this assignment a little harder. I would like you to practice mindfulness while you eat. This means you will get off of technology, get away from your work, and try your best not to talk about work or stressful topics while you eat.

How you eat is just as important and *what* and *when* you eat. If you are thinking about your cases and you are stressed out, you are not able to digest your food properly because the body is constricted and in defense mode. According to Ayurveda, you should eat all your meals in a peaceful place and only have peaceful conversation. It is best not to talk that much while eating because extra air will go in with the food. And eating should not take that long either. Your practice should be that you get your food, you eat it mindfully, and then afterward you take a break from eating for a couple of hours (fasting) and let your body digest the food. (Snacking between meals can upset the digestive system. If you eat enough food at meals, you will be satisfied until the next meal. But that will come later for you. For now, you should eat whenever you need to nourish yourself.)

I understand that you have lunch work meetings where talking about work while eating is common, so just do your best on those days. Maybe a portion of your lunch or meeting could be more mindful. When possible, please try to pull yourself away from your work for your lunch break. Only have pleasant conversations if you are going to talk. You may have forgotten that you are a whole person and can have conversations not about the law or your cases or politics. And then actually take the time to eat your food. Yes, eating is a social activity, and ideally, we would be with people we love and take our time to enjoy a nourishing home-cooked meal in the middle of the day, as many cultures do. But in some modern Western cultures, lunch breaks are going extinct.

Further, if you don't eat lunch when you should, or under stressful conditions (i.e., while working), you will eat more at dinner since you are not satisfied or nourished. Eating heavy late dinners is the cause of many common digestive issues. These problems have become normalized, but if we pay attention to our eating habits, the digestive problems can go away. Just imagine all the time you could save by not having stomachaches! As a bonus, this practice of eating a proper meal at lunchtime will definitely help your weight-loss goals. The benefits of eating lunch properly are exponential.

Try taking a real lunch break for the week, along with your 6 minutes of meditation. We have to feed ourselves! People are getting sick because they are not feeding themselves the right things, not taking breaks, and eating when they are upset or on the go. Food becomes our body—it literally becomes our cells—so it is not just for pleasure and entertainment, you are taking it into your body for nourishment. Of course, food should be pleasurable and have a loving and nurturing quality. When you cook food and you feed other people, you put love into the food. You have to lovingly feed yourself too.

To review, the homework for the next week is that you are going to continue to meditate every day for 6 minutes. Separately, you are going to take a lunch break from your work and eat nourishing food for at least 12 minutes each day.

The feedback I get from the lawyers doing this program is that, when they are doing it, they enjoy it. Their challenge is being regimented about it. I have also heard that, while it may be hard, "Hard produces results." Incorporating the New Billable Hour into your routine will get harder as you work your way to the whole hour, but then it gets easier because you will be able to double-bill. It gets better. Stick with it. When you bring these beneficial things into your life, a lot of the "time wasters" fall away and even more time opens up. This allows for increased productivity and ease in your work and life.

You may be thinking that this is difficult because client meetings run into your lunch time. And the planning ahead is a challenge because of work demands. Maybe you are a parent and you pack everyone else's lunch but not your own. Remember, if you eat a proper lunch, you won't feel hungry at the end of the day with a stomachache. If that were true for you, what could that open up? Maybe you could go work out, or go for a walk. You could be feel more at ease and ultimately more productive.

Andrew is a lawyer who was suffering from regular bouts of abdominal pain, vomiting, and other digestive distress. Sometimes he would have such excruciating pain in his gut that he would have to go to the emergency room. This would happen several times a year and put him out of commission for at least a week. The doctors could not tell him what was wrong; they would just give him medication to dull the pain and send him home. He would have to recover on his own, only to go through the same cycle again a few months later. Andrew came to me because he knew that I helped lawyers with their well-being and he was interested in Ayurveda as an alternative. He wanted to get any relief from his pain and, more importantly, lost time and productivity at work.

When I pressed him about exactly when these incidents would happen, he admitted that they were related to stress and overworking. And when Andrew is stressed or working a lot, he does not take care of his wellness. Andrew does not take the time to eat a proper lunch, and then is so hungry at the end of the day that he ends up eating fast food late at night. This habit triggers stomach upsets that keep him up at night. I worked with him to slowly change his routine to eat a bigger regular lunch, and his symptoms got better. Because he felt better, he was able to focus more on being a lawyer. He didn't miss as much time from work, and his productivity increased.

Of course, just eating lunch is no substitute for medical attention. And Andrew's condition is severe. I am sharing Andrew's story to remind you that your digestive system is sensitive and must be cared for. This is the essence of self-care. If your body is telling you that you need food in the middle of the day, you must honor that signal. Ignoring it over time can lead to health problems that may not be easily reversed. But changing your habits is possible if you make that choice to try something new.

The good news is that taking a lunch break from work and technology for only 12 minutes per day away will keep your gut healthy and happy. A healthy gut both directly and indirectly relates to your brain, clarity, focus, and productivity. There is research about the "brain-gut connection," the communication between your brain and your enteric nervous system (ENS), which resides in your digestive system. Gut problems such as irritable bowel syndrome (IBS) are often related to depression and anxiety. In sum, you can take care of your gut *and* brain with the daily practice of a 12-minute mindful lunch break. The time for this lifestyle improvement is now.

Chapter 6
Lesson Three:
Morning Routine, .2 Hours

If you win the morning, you win the day.
–Tim Ferriss, author of *The 4-Hour Workweek*

Now that you have successfully added meditation and a lunch break to your workday, you will learn how to make some changes at home. Even though the lessons are not linear, there is a reason I have asked you to incorporate your lunch break before incorporating your morning routine. The lunch break is done during the work day and relatively easy to achieve. But this next lesson is about your personal morning routine; you may have to make some significant changes in your personal life.

The most successful people on the planet swear by a morning routine. Having a powerful morning routine sets your day up for success and productivity. Starting your day mindfully grounds you and inspires you to stay focused on what is really important. If you don't believe me, think about those days (and they are necessary) when you have no routine or structure and you basically lose the day because you don't know where to start.

Just like the other lessons, the morning routine does not have to take much time. The routine should be practiced daily, even when you are on vacation and not going to the office. It does not matter so much *what* is in your routine, as long as you have one. Waking up and starting the day is so much easier when you have a go-to routine that does not require thought and planning. For your New Billable Hour, your morning routine need only be about 12 minutes, or .2 hours.

Your morning routines will change over time as you learn more about your unique needs. But it is important to create one now and practice having one before you change it around. To receive maximum benefit from your short morning routine, postpone engaging with technology, including media, phone, internet, and news, until you have completed your routine. If you get on your phone, checking email and social media first thing in the morning, you are simply turning on your anxiety right after waking up and making it difficult to turn it off all day. And that is why it's so hard to meditate later. What you do in the first part of your day sets the stage for the rest of your day. If you are turning *on* your racing mind first thing, it will be difficult to find the peace and clarity you seek. You want to enter the day with calm and clarity so that you can respond meaningfully instead of merely reacting to what comes at you.

Deciding on your first morning routine is a fun and creative task. There are many options and examples suggested by the productivity experts and by the ancient wisdom of Ayurveda. In creating your own routine, make sure it (1) is simple, (2) sets you up for the day, and (3) is positive. Here are some examples of what you can include in your 12-minute morning routine:

1. Make your bed
2. Hydrate (drink some water)
3. Connect with loved ones
4. Take care of your personal hygiene
5. Pack your lunch
6. Do some quick exercise to get your blood pumping
7. Read something inspirational or invoke a daily affirmation
8. Write in a journal
9. Create a (very short) to-do list to plan the day
10. Meditate or practice gratitude
11. Focus on your personal vision statement for your life

If you are reading this book, your current lifestyle probably is not working for you. You may think that, in order to be more productive and bill more hours, you need to start working before you even get out of bed. This is all too common for lawyers. You start the day reacting to others' needs instead of owning the day and setting your intentions. Then you suffer from anxiety, stress, and general discontent with your life. It is time to make a change.

It will be challenging to change your conditioned habit of jumping into work and starting the day with chaos. Your mind and body will resist this change because you are used to your current habit. So the key here is to try something new and see how you feel. This program is meant to be an experiment on yourself, so you can see how to increase your productivity and have more balance.

Joanna, a lawyer, was a participant in a group program I facilitated teaching the principles of the New Billable Hour. When she started the program, she reported being anxious and feeling responsible for her clients to her detriment. She wanted help to feel less stressed and frazzled during the day, to be more able focus on her work, and to leave it behind when she was not working. When I taught this particular lesson, she exclaimed, "Is this a trick?" She said she already had things she did for her self-care in the mornings, so this would be no problem for her. Joanna set out to continue her daily routine of working out, making her lunch, and planning her day. But, when the group met again, she said it was actually difficult to get in a consistent routine and change her habit of listening to the news right when she woke up. She also realized that she was on her phone and checking her emails in the midst of her morning activities.

Joanna's first move was to look at her phone when she woke up. Then she was "on," as she explained. She was catching up with the events of the world, her networks, and her clients first thing in the morning. While she thought she was being productive by getting to work right away, she was open to another way of doing things.

So Joanna followed the program and avoided the news and her email in the mornings. She focused on getting dressed for her workout, spending time with her family, and taking care of her hygiene *without* engaging in any media or lawyer work. This was a big change for Joanna.

Establishing her morning routine *before* starting her work day shifted Joanna's relationship to her work. She started with 12 minutes and then decided to spend several hours doing what she needed to ground herself for the day, including going to the gym. At first, she did feel guilty for not working in those morning hours. But that guilt did not last long. Once she saw her anxiety decrease and saw herself feel "less frazzled" during the day, Joanna knew that structuring her day this way meant she could focus more and be more efficient and productive during her 8-10-hour workday. She knows now that, in order to be more productive, she cannot let work "creep up" into her morning routine.

I am sure you know by now that positive thinking has been scientifically proven to expand your mind and open up possibilities. Positivity researcher Dr. Barbara L. Fredrickson has found that, while negativity breeds damaging emotions that deplete you, a positive mental state can broaden your mind. Increased productivity depends on a broad and open mind. So if you carelessly start your day in chaos and reactivity, that is where your mind will stay. But if you intentionally start the day with a morning routine that is positive, your mind will be open. Further, Ayurveda supports a morning ritual as the keystone for good health and longevity. Are you ready to jump-start your day and your life in just 12 minutes? If yes, you can start your morning routine tomorrow!

Chapter 7
Lesson Four:
Night Routine, .2 Hours

A ruffled mind makes a restless pillow.
–Charlotte Brontë

George is a lawyer and suffers from sleeplessness. According to him, "Sleeping is not a sure thing." The idea of having a long night's sleep just doesn't exist for him. He usually goes to bed between 9 to 10 p.m. and gets up around 5 a.m. But he wakes up several times during the night, thinking about cases, clients, things that he forgot to do, and things that he *didn't* forget to do. It has become his norm to wake up already thinking stressful thoughts. Then, since he does not sleep well, he is tired the next day. This cycle is getting worse and worse for him.

He went to his doctor about his sleep issues and was prescribed medication. George is mortified that he has to take these pills and does not want to become an addict. So he will sometimes skip a night and not take the pill. But then he does not sleep. He used to sleep well. He remembers that the first time he had difficulty with sleep was at the end of law school, when he did not sleep for three days. Since then, sleep has been variable for him. But, in the last few years, he has realized he has a problem and is willing to admit it.

Most lawyers I talk to experience this kind of insomnia—waking up in the early hours of the morning, like 2 or 3 a.m., thinking of stressful topics. I also suffer from this insomnia, especially when I don't practice a night routine. A routine at night is just as important as, if not more important than, your morning routine. Just as your morning routine sets up your day, your night routine sets up your night! And by your night, I mean your sleep. A productive tomorrow begins tonight. We can agree that, with a good's night's sleep, the next day you will be more clear, focused, and productive.

Modern life has blessed us with electricity, electronics, and lots of screens to capture our attention. You may be reading this book right now on a screen at night! I get it; everyone is doing it. That's just the way it is. There is so much to do during our day that it spills over into the night. I know many lawyers who are doing serious, brain-taxing work at night and it feels like there is no escape from it.

This lesson is to create a 12-minute nightly routine where you unplug from all technology and wind down from your day. The goal is to set yourself up for more restful sleep.

Here are some ideas of what you can include in your night routine:

1. Practice restorative yoga or stretching
2. Drink warm milk or herbal tea
3. Journal about your day or what you are grateful for
4. Write down a to-do list for the next day with a positive attitude

5. Read a book with positive messages
6. Cover your eyes with an eye pillow (or cool your eyes with rose water)
7. Listen to soothing music
8. Draw, paint, or engage in another artistic activity
9. Take a bath, shower, sauna, or hot tub
10. Meditate

It is most important to end each day in a relaxing way, and best to do the same 1-3 activities every day. As I explained about the morning routine, doing the same thing has benefits because you don't have to think about what to do, and routines are very grounding for the nervous system. If you can relax the mind and nerves, your body will be able to rest since you will feel safe.

What can you do to show your body you are safe so it can rest? I am sure that your normal lawyer activities are not it. Thinking about the law and clients just wakes up your nervous system. No wonder you wake up in the middle of the night ready to fight! You have bedtime routines for your children, but you bombard yourself with data and stress right before you go to sleep. It is no wonder most lawyers have trouble sleeping. I have heard so many times from lawyers that, if they could just figure out sleep, everything else would fall into place. With good rest, we function better, have more clarity, and are more productive.

You get to do whatever you want during the day; it's just these 12 minutes on either end that are going to change your life forever. You will have more time, productivity, and joy during your days! 12 minutes before you go to sleep, please turn off your electronics. This is going to be hard, but you have done harder things. Engage in some type of ceremony of putting the media and your connection to everything to bed. Everything will be there for you after your morning routine tomorrow. You are a lawyer, and you need to be rested so you can do your lawyer work the next day. You will do better, more efficient work if you are rested. If an emergency happens during the night, you will be able to respond in the morning. Your brain will be working properly and you will not waste time doing other things.

The morning routine is about getting things done and being active. The night routine is about relaxing and winding down. You know how at night you feel tired and you push through? Then you can't sleep, and like George, you need aids to help you do it? You don't need to change your bedtimes right now. First, do these 12 minutes of a night routine and see how it affects your sleep.

The night routine is specific to you and what will help *you* sleep. One participant in my program said that, if she starts to read, she will stay up for hours reading. For her, reading at night is not a good idea to promote better sleep. Journaling is a nice thing to try with this lesson if it is new to you. Some prompts are: "What am I grateful for about this day?" or "My progress with the New Billable Hour." It doesn't matter what you write down. No one is going to see it. The night routine is a tool to help bring calm and put your day to bed.

This lesson may be difficult for you. But having some downtime at the end of the day is crucial for naturally calming your mind and body, which will allow you to rest.

Resting increases our productivity by benefiting our thinking and creativity. Alex Soojung-Kim Pang, author of *Rest: Why You Get More Done When You Work Less*, explains that, when you sleep, your body shifts into maintenance mode and devotes itself to storing energy, fixing or replacing damaged cells, and growing, while your brain cleans out toxins, processes the day's experiences, and can work on problems that have been burdening your waking mind. You must have experienced the clarity you gain after "sleeping on" a problem.

On the contrary, *lack of sleep* can lead to a weakened immune system, impaired decision-making, diminished ability to learn new skills, decreased reaction time, mental health imbalances, and a propensity to make mistakes. This list is so relevant to lawyers, because the stakes are high in your work. Even one small mistake can mean disastrous consequences for your client *and* you. In a culture that says productivity means sacrificing rest, you are putting yourself and your client at risk by not prioritizing your sleep.

The good news is that a short, consistent, 12-minute night routine will mean better sleep. Sufficient sleep will lead to an increase in immunity, decision-making, ability to learn, reaction time, and productivity. Since you already have a positive and energizing morning routine, simply add in your calming night routine tonight!

Chapter 8
Lesson Five:
Movement (with Breath), .2 hours

Nothing is more revealing than movement.
–Martha Graham

Originally, this was going to be the yoga chapter, because I love yoga. A lot. It has changed my life in so many ways, and continues to do so. Could I make this step practicing 12 minutes of yoga every day? Heck yes! There are great videos online that are 10-15 minutes long and appropriate for all levels. That small amount of yoga each day will cure all that ails you! The magic of yoga is that this ancient practice purposefully focuses on connecting movement with breath. Integrating your body with life-giving breath brings you into the present moment. Being in this moment, as we see from sitting meditation, brings you clarity, focus, and increased productivity.

But perhaps you don't want to do yoga, or perhaps you want to exercise in a different way. That is acceptable and I will allow it. In my consulting with lawyers, many already practice yoga, and many have other ways they move their bodies. Eric, who works for a large law firm, proclaimed to me when we talked, "I have no scientific basis for this, but moving your body changes your brain chemistry in a positive way!" He didn't always feel this way. Eric suffered through physical education in school and didn't like exercise growing up. Before he discovered running, he weighed 366 pounds and was depressed. He felt lethargy and malaise and didn't want to get out of bed. His solo law practice was, according to him, "tanking" for three years, and he had passing thoughts of suicide.

While everything felt like it was falling apart around him, he found the "Couch to 5K" mobile application and started running on the treadmill at his apartment complex. Eric shared with me that, at the end of his first session, he experienced clarity of mind that he didn't have before. He got out of his fog, took a long hard look at his life, and started to make changes. At first, he just ran; then over time, he started to think about his breath and integrate it with his running cadence. He now breathes in through his nose and out through his mouth while counting his footfalls.

I share this detail with you because I thought only yoga did this for you. So instead of being the yoga lesson, this lesson became about movement with breath more generally. Since you may already have a running (or some other kind of exercise) practice, the lesson is to focus on your breath for at least 12 minutes during that workout. This generally means unplugging from your music and podcasts, much like in all the previous lessons. Just notice your breath and maybe move with your breath.

However, if you don't already have movement or exercise as part of your day, now is the time to incorporate it. In that case, this week's lesson is to add 12 minutes to your day of moving your body. You can do a yoga video, go to the gym, go for a run, or walk, dance, or do anything you find fun. I hear from lawyers that they have activities they enjoy doing, like running, biking, walking, and other sports, but they do not do them "as much as they'd like to." I also hear that it takes too much time during the workday to go exercise. Ultimately, your movement can be incorporated into your morning or night routine.

As a lawyer, you carry a lot of your stress and pain in your physical body. Moving your body with your breath helps clear this muscle tension. If you don't address the tension, then it will show up as other health issues or illness, which will lead to more pain. Most people are in pain and are trying to mask or avoid it as opposed to experiencing it and allowing it to move through. If you can learn to move your body without distractions, the pain will move along.

Furthermore, in this day and age, we are really disconnected from our bodies. As a lawyer, you are more in your head than your body. Movement allows you to drop out of your head and into your body.

It turns out that Eric was right; regular exercise does change your brain. Exercise benefits the size of the brain as well as the beneficial chemicals it produces. Regular movement slows neural degeneration, reduces stress, improves sleep, and improves creative energy. Ron Friedman, PhD, author of *The Best Place to Work: The Art and Science of Creating an Extraordinary Workplace*, reviews studies that indicate that our mental firepower is directly linked to our physical regimen. He confirms that incorporating regular exercise into your routine results in the following benefits: improved concentration, sharper memory, faster learning, prolonged mental stamina, enhanced creativity, lower stress, and elevated mood.

By incorporating at least 12 minutes of movement into your day, you are now at 54 minutes of the New Billable Hour. Remember this is all aspirational, and if you have a "bad day," just start over the next day. You are learning new lifelong tools you can rely on when you need them. But, to increase your available time, energy, and productivity, it is imperative to prioritize these activities every day.

Chapter 9
Lesson Six:
Connecting with Nature, .1 Hours

Look deep into nature, and then you will understand everything better.

–Albert Einstein

As I write this chapter, I have to admit I would rather be watching the sky. Being in nature does something to me that is indescribable. It feels like my whole being is being rebooted. Whether you like to move your body or not, I know that you *are moved* by the beauty of nature. How can it be so perfect? How can the clouds moving in the sky be so grand? No matter whether I am in a city or in the mountain paradise where I live, I find the sky envelops me. When I am on the move, I try to notice the sky and see what it is doing. I am in awe of how I can lose my sense of time and space just by noticing nature.

The last 6 minutes of the New Billable Hour are for connecting with nature. This is the prize at the end of this journey, because deep down you want to do this, but you think you don't have time during your regular day. You go on fabulous vacations to beautiful natural places and soak it in for days or weeks. This is fine; keep doing that. But what about doing it every day? This lesson is to connect with nature in whatever way you can for 6 minutes daily. If you can, please get outside and go to a park, the ocean, the forest, or the desert and really connect with the environment around you. If that is not possible, you can also have a garden or a plant that you pay attention to and take care of every day. This can be indoors or on a patio or a balcony.

If even that is not possible, then look out a window and watch the sky. Simply find a window and sit for about 6 minutes and look at the sky, watching clouds go by (if you are lucky enough to see that!). Spending time with animals is another way to connect with nature. Take just 6 minutes to give your pet undivided attention and notice the connection.

During your time with nature, you don't have to worry about a structured meditation or any of the other things we have worked on. Just be present and let nature do its thing around you. It is so powerful that you don't need to do much.

If none of the above is possible for you, try looking at photos and videos of nature instead. It will be more effective to look at photos and videos that you took yourself. There was a reason for taking them, after all. They serve as memory triggers of the feelings you had when you were in that moment. If you go to a place that really moves you, take a photo and then go back to it. When I was recently traveling in a city, I really missed my mountain home. Then I happened to see a photo I took of my stunning forest view and I immediately felt transported home and to a more relaxed state. Listening to nature sounds could also work for you.

This lesson can be done any time of day as long as you prioritize it. While incorporating this last lesson of the New Billable Hour, I don't want you to "double-bill" yet. But, as you incorporate your routines into your life, you may want to do any of the other lessons while connecting with nature.

Samantha is a lawyer who has the common problem of feeling like she works too much and does not have time for what is important to her. She lives steps from the ocean, so she committed herself to watch the sun rise every morning and posting photos of the beauty on social media. The photos are breathtaking and interesting to see throughout the year. She has declared herself the "sun ambassador" and advocate for nature. When Samantha sees the ocean, her heart pours out with gratitude. She told me that, when she is at the beach, she is in the moment because nature is a "miracle to witness." She sees the ocean changing; sometimes it is chaotic and sometimes calm. Samantha feels hopeful when she experiences this because it mirrors changes in her own life, and she feels like "all is well."

Whether you are an "outdoorsy" person or prefer to be inside, connecting with nature will increase your productivity. Studies show that being in nature improves short term memory, sparks inspiration, decreases stress levels, increases concentration skills, boosts positivity, enhances creative functions, and increases mindfulness.

Have you heard of "forest bathing"? Not really a bath, this term originating from Japan means walking in the forest for the health benefits. And in the US, the media is highlighting the research from Japan to promote going into nature as a way to get away from work and de-stress.

Please consider this last lesson of only 6 minutes or .1 hours per day of connecting with nature a *gift*, a reward for your hard work doing the New Billable Hour. And you will be further rewarded with more billable hours, increased productivity, and balance in your life.

Chapter 10
Competence and Diligence

The leading rule for the lawyer, as for the man of every calling, is diligence.

–Abraham Lincoln

Y ou are close to the end of the book, and maybe you are wondering when you will be billing more hours, or being more productive, or have that work-life balance. It takes practice, repetition, and mastery of the New Billable Hour over six weeks to truly begin to see the difference. I've had lawyers go through the program and, after six weeks, see major shifts in their lives as a result of committed and focused daily practice. This isn't something you can do one day and not the next—you have to be consistent. While you may not notice the shifts that are happening—and they are—pay attention to the next time you interact with a client or are met with a stressful situation. You now have the tools of the New Billable Hour. You may have tried them out. You may have realized that you are doing many of these activities already and see them differently. I imagine there were several "aha!" moments as you read this book about how your daily habits and routines can affect your productivity and ability to focus.

I titled this chapter "Competence and Diligence" to remind you of your duties as a lawyer that I know you take seriously. You are committed to giving your clients your best work and efforts. You understand that you have legal and ethical obligations to perform this work with the highest integrity. And to make that happen, to be the best lawyer you can be, you must give yourself this same level of competence and diligence.

Since I know you have discipline, I know you can do this. I know you can push through and do the lessons because you know it is what you need. You know you need this New Billable Hour to achieve results. You have a responsibility to step up, raise your hand, and advocate for your life to be different. I know you want a life where you're an amazing attorney who bills hours easily, is super-productive most of the time, and who has a work-life balance that makes you want to shout from the rooftops. I know you want this, and I know you believe you can achieve it.

It is your time to shine and your responsibility to make this happen. I know you can do it. You can reread this book and implement the lessons into your life one by one. And when you fall off the wagon (which you will) and forget, you can always come back to this book to remember. *The New Billable Hour* is my gift to you. Please accept it from my heart and share it generously.

Conclusion

At his best, man is the noblest of all animals;
separated from law and justice, he is the worst.
–Aristotle

L awyers are modern-day healers. You are also a warrior fighting for justice for your clients. It does not matter what kind of law you practice. If you practice law and have a client, that client is going through some type of conflict or transition, and you are called upon to get him through his problem. In fact, your calling is so strong that you do that above all else. And you truly believe this. You take your responsibility to serve your clients seriously. You take on your clients' problems as your own and work hard to solve them.

Your clients are suffering in some way, and you are called to help them. This calling is a true honor and privilege. Your clients trust you to be their expert guide to get to the other side of their problems. With this responsibility comes intense power. You can choose to use your position to hurt and take advantage of people, or you can choose to use your power to help your clients and the planet get to the next level. You are here for a purpose, and being a lawyer is a crucial part of your path and journey.

There can be no regrets in this complex life. It is more beneficial to accept that you were chosen to take on this role for however long you take it. I wish for you to embrace this role as lawyer. I wish for you to make small, enduring changes in your life and perspective that will ripple out into the profession. I wish for you to advocate for change and stand up for your colleagues who are feeling alone and turning to choices that could destroy their careers and lives. I wish for you to listen to the new lawyers and law students and help them change the profession. I wish for you to collaborate more with each other so you don't feel so alone.

If now, or sometime in the future, you decide to change the course of your life, I wish you a happy transition. I wish for you to be proud and honored to have served in the trenches as a practicing lawyer. I wish for you no shame or regret or feelings of failure. I wish for you to use your gifts and experience in a meaningful way.

And if you are just trying to figure out what to do tomorrow, my wish is that you pick up this book and start to implement the New Billable Hour with lesson one. Then after a week, add another lesson. Add another lesson each week until you understand all six. After that I wish for you to try every day to implement the New Billable Hour as best you can. Then, no matter how it went, I wish for you to start over in implementing the New Billable Hour again the next day. I wish for you no shame or judgment, no matter what you accomplish each day with the New Billable Hour. I wish for you a clean slate every day when you open your eyes, to implement the New Billable Hour with a beginner's mind. Your wealth is your time and awareness. Dear lawyer, I wish for you much wealth, increased productivity, and balance beyond your wildest dreams.

Acknowledgments

I have wanted to write this book for a long time. And when I would shelve the idea, the whisper telling me to help lawyers find more time and balance in their lives just got louder. Inspiration for *The New Billable Hour* model came from studying the deep ancient wisdom of Ayurveda and the work of Deepak Chopra, combined with the modern productivity hacks for lifestyle design from Tim Ferriss. These mentors have, through their books, helped me master ways to maintain balance while making a difference in other people's lives. I am honored to share these methods with you. Right here and right now, we are starting a movement to change the legal profession by gaining control of our time and how we (and others) see it.

While I am at a new beginning in my life, this book is the culmination of my journey thus far. I want to thank all my teachers, mentors, colleagues, students, and friends who have shaped me, made me think, and pushed me to the next level. Thank you to Angie Boissevain, my Zen teacher, mentor, and friend. You have taught and shown me so much about being a strong modern woman and setting boundaries. Speaking of boundaries, all of my yoga teachers have been instrumental in holding space and guiding me to open up in ways I never imagined. Thank you, Noell Clark, for showing me how to always teach yoga with great integrity. And deep bows to Erika Abrahamian, for most literally "having my back" and allowing me to blossom in your healing hands. This book is just the beginning of allowing myself to be seen and to share my message. Thank you, Angela Lauria and the Author Incubator team, for making this possible and launching me. And Ron Stotts, I will always appreciate your faith and trust in me to remember who I really am.

To the Morgan James Publishing team: Special thanks to David Hancock, CEO & Founder for believing in me and my message. To my Author Relations Manager, Margo Toulouse, thanks for making the process seamless and easy. Many more thanks to everyone else, but especially Jim Howard, Bethany Marshall, and Nickcole Watkins.

To the lawyers who trusted me and signed up for the first New Billable Hour live group program before I had even created it—Cory Caouette, Jeraline Singh Edwards, Jesse Lloyd, Irma Pérez, and Hardeep Sull—thank you for actively participating in the program that formed the foundation of this book. Your respect, commitment, humor, curiosity, and fearlessness made this journey possible. You are each leaders in this movement toward changing the legal profession into a more balanced one. I commend you for taking this leap and I wish for all your dreams to come true.

The lawyer case studies in this book are melded characters created from individual clients and colleagues who have given me permission to share their stories. All names have been changed to protect confidentiality. I want to express profound gratitude to all who shared their experiences for this book.

About the Author

Ritu Goswamy, Esq., is a lawyer and productivity consultant. Her training as a lawyer, social worker, entrepreneur, yoga instructor, and Ayurvedic health counselor have helped her understand the modern demands on lawyers and their desire for more balance. She strives to combine ancient wisdom with modern time hacks to help other lawyers create work-life balance without having to leave the profession.

Ritu is the creator of the New Billable Hour™ system, which helps lawyers increase their productivity by billing themselves first. She teaches this system directly to lawyers in a way that is engaging, fun, and practical. By prioritizing your needs in an efficient way, you are able to then respond to other demands on your time. Ritu's philosophy is to shift from the reactive training we have as lawyers to live more intentionally and ultimately have a bigger impact in all aspects of our lives.

Ritu holds a bachelor of arts in psychology from Barnard College and a juris doctorate and master of social work from Boston College. She is a Registered Yoga Teacher with Yoga Alliance and a certified Ayurvedic Health Counselor. While Ritu relishes her solitude living in the Santa Cruz Mountains, she also engages with the innovative vibrations of Silicon Valley just over the hill.

Website: www.newbillablehour.com

Email: ritu@newbillablehour.com

Linkedin: http://www.linkedin.com/in/ritu-goswamy/

Facebook: www.facebook.com/ritugo

Thank You

Congratulations on taking the first step to look at the billable hour in a new way! This book starts your journey toward learning how to be more productive and get the most out of all your hours.

For more resources and links to scientific studies related to increased productivity, visit www.newbillablehour.com/resources.

To help you implement these lessons into your life, you can download a free printable checklist of the 6 lessons of the New Billable Hour at www.newbillablehour.com/checklist.

Have you wondered how productive you actually are with your billable hours? As a bonus, I invite you to take my free online quiz to find out at www.newbillablehour. com/quiz.

If you want to continue the conversation, you can also email me directly at ritu@newbillablehour.com.

Wishing you a productive and rewarding legal career,

Ritu Goswamy, Esq.

Morgan James
Speakers Group

We connect Morgan James published
authors with live and online events
and audiences who will benefit
from their expertise.

Morgan James makes all of our titles available
through the Library for All Charity Organization.

www.LibraryForAll.org

.

CPSIA information can be obtained
at www.ICGtesting.com
Printed in the USA
BVHW031340190719
553928BV00003B/587/P

9 781642 791273